D0547879

THE *ALTERNATIVE* BODY BOOK

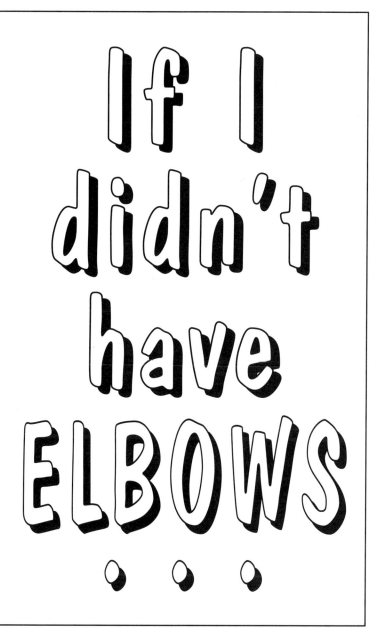

If I didn't have ELBOWS...

WRITTEN BY SANDI TOKSVIG
ILLUSTRATED BY DAVID MELLING

Medical Consultant — Dr. Tony Smith
Deputy Editor of the British Medical Journal and Medical Editor
of the British Medical Association's Family Doctor Publications

For **Jesse, Meg and Ted** – S.T.

For **Sarah, Suzy, Anna and Ambreen,**
for making sure that the light at the end of
the tunnel always had a fresh bulb — D.M.

THE ALTERNATIVE BODY BOOK

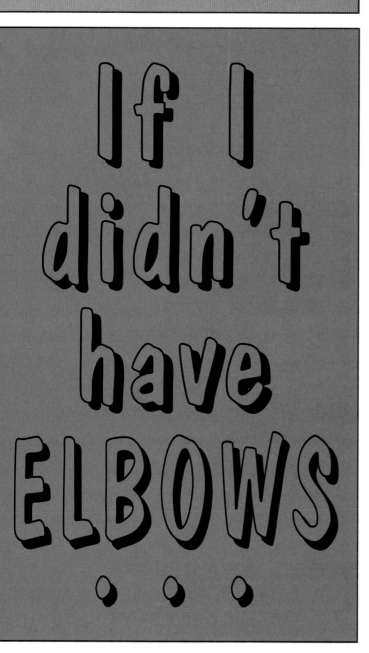

If I didn't have ELBOWS . . .

WRITTEN BY **SANDI TOKSVIG**
ILLUSTRATED BY **DAVID MELLING**

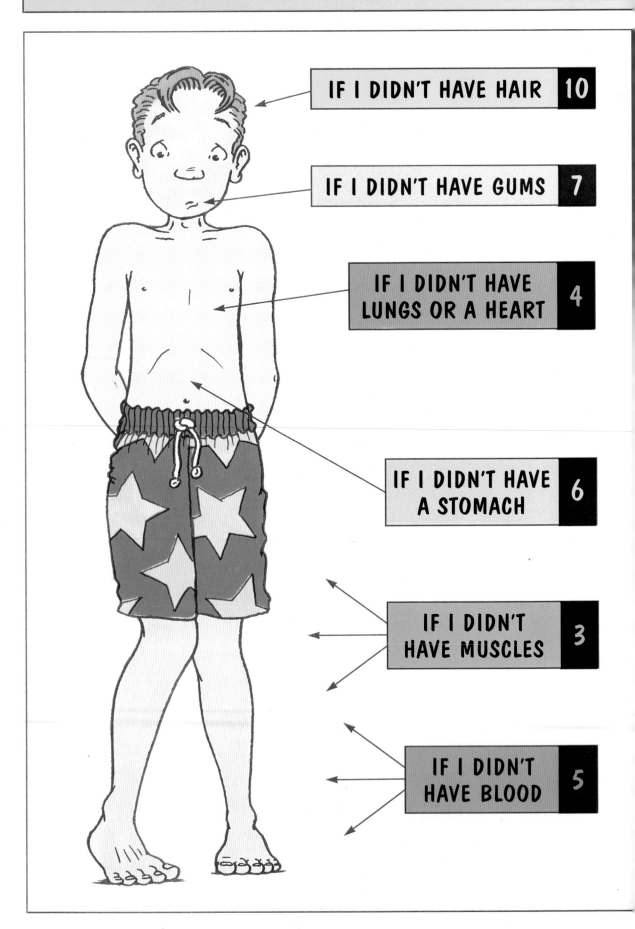

YOU WOULDN'T KNOW WHAT YOU COULD READ ABOUT IN THIS BOOK

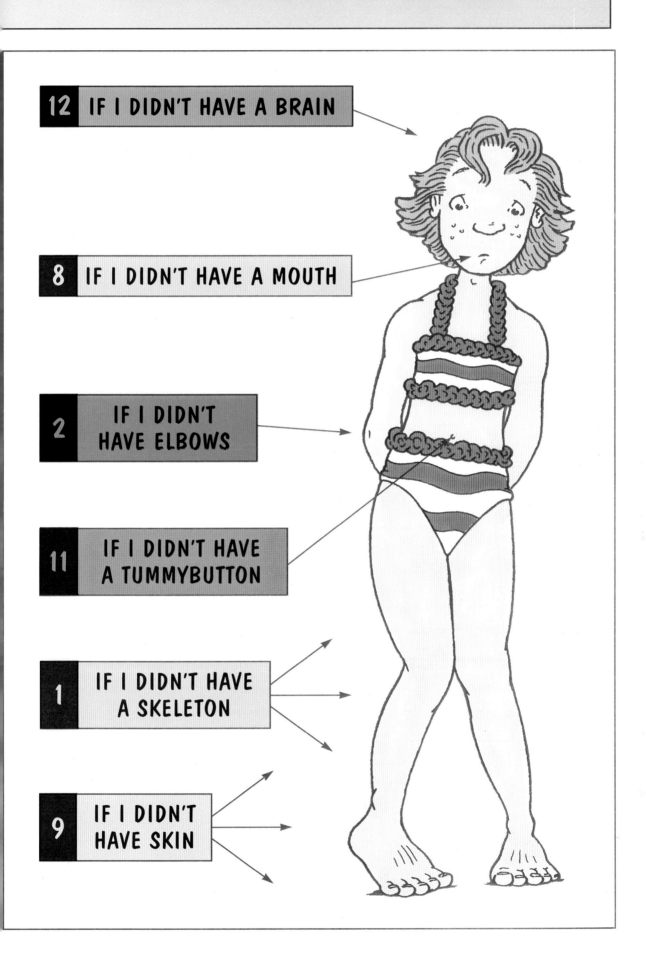

12 IF I DIDN'T HAVE A BRAIN

8 IF I DIDN'T HAVE A MOUTH

2 IF I DIDN'T HAVE ELBOWS

11 IF I DIDN'T HAVE A TUMMYBUTTON

1 IF I DIDN'T HAVE A SKELETON

9 IF I DIDN'T HAVE SKIN

Your skeleton has 206 bones. There are 27 bones in the human hand alone...

but that doesn't make everyone a good pianist.

A sparrow has more bones than a giraffe!

When you were a baby, your bones were mostly made of rubbery cartilage. As you got older, calcium helped make them harder.

MY SKELETON HOLDS MY BODY UP.

1

If I didn't have a SKELETON...

I'D HAVE TO WEAR MY BASEBALL KIT FOR ALL MY GAMES!

A lobster has extra protection — its skeleton is on the outside. When it has grown too big for its shell, the shell falls off. It takes a month to grow a new one — this is a scary time for lobsters!

I'D HAVE TROUBLE CARRYING A RUCKSACK.

Porcupines have quills for extra protection. But they have to be careful when feeding their babies!

An octopus doesn't have a skeleton, but the water helps to hold it up so it doesn't matter that it is all floppy.

Then again...
an octopus has never won Wimbledon!

MY SKELETON PROTECTS THE SOFT AND IMPORTANT PARTS OF MY BODY LIKE MY LUNGS.

GRANNY COULDN'T KEEP TELLING ME TO SIT UP STRAIGHT.

Some snakes have very unusual jaws.

They can unhook the joints to open their mouths very wide and swallow big things. It's a good idea to stay away from snakes who are ready for dinner!

EXCEPT FOR MY JAW, THE JOINTS IN MY SKULL DON'T MOVE.

Your neck is a pivot joint — it lets your head move 180° from side to side. It's just as well you can't look backwards or you might trip up when you walk.

Oysters have shells instead of skeletons. The shells are hinged but oysters have no legs so they never leave home!

MY ELBOW IS THE JOINT THAT ALLOWS MY ARM TO BEND.

MY SKELETON IS FLEXIBLE

2

If I didn't have ELBOWS.

I'D HAVE
A LOUSY BACKHAND
IN TENNIS.

I'D ALWAYS BE POURING DRINKS DOWN MY BACK.

BECAUSE IT IS JOINTED.

Your elbow and knee are hinge joints. Just like door hinges, they allow your arms and legs to go forward and backward.

If you couldn't bend your knees, you couldn't sit down. This would be rather tiring!

BONES CAN'T BEND, BUT WHEN TWO BONES MEET THEY FORM A FLEXIBLE CONNECTION CALLED A JOINT.

I'D HAVE TO GIVE UP ARM WRESTLING!

Your hip and shoulder are ball-and-socket joints. These give an incredible amount of movement.

If you didn't have so many different types of joints, you wouldn't be able to scratch your shoulder and you'd probably be useless at swimming.

Fish contract their muscles in waves along the length of their bodies. This is how they swim through the water.

Cuttlefish use their muscles to contract or expand bags of colour in their skin. This helps them to change colour very quickly so they match their surroundings.

Pianos have legs, but no muscles — they are rubbish at the 100 metres.

I MOVE MY JOINTS WITH MUSCLES

3

If I didn't have MUSCLES

MY HEART IS A SPECIAL MUSCLE. IT PUMPS BLOOD AROUND MY BODY.

The squid has muscles, but no legs. It moves by jet propulsion: it pulls water into its body, then squeezes its muscles to force it out again. This makes it move.

Woodpeckers have special muscles in their heads that absorb the shock when they peck trees.

We don't have these muscles, so banging your head on wood could be very painful!

MY EYE HAS SIX MUSCLES WHICH HELP ME TO LOOK AROUND.

It takes more muscles to frown than it does to smile — so save energy and smile!

I'D ALWAYS STARE STRAIGHT AHEAD.

THAT I CAN CONTROL.

I HAVE THREE DIFFERENT TYPES OF MUSCLES. SKELETAL MUSCLES ARE ONE TYPE — THEY HELP ME TO MOVE. I HAVE TO THINK TO CONTROL THEM.

Cats have very elastic muscles in their backs so they can twist quickly and nearly always land on their feet if they fall or are dropped. Cats prefer if you do not test this.

For walking you need to use as many as 200 different muscles. Makes you want to sit down just thinking about it!

SMOOTH MUSCLES SQUEEZE FOOD ALONG MY INSIDES. I DON'T HAVE TO THINK ABOUT THEM, THEY WORK BY THEMSELVES.

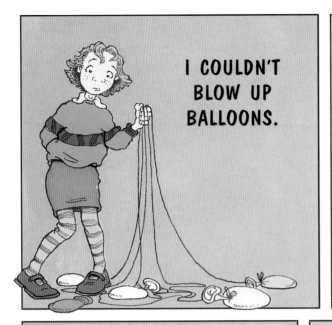

I COULDN'T BLOW UP BALLOONS.

Fish don't have lungs so they can't live on land. But they can live underwater because they breathe through gills at the side of their heads.

I NEED OXYGEN TO LIVE. MY LUNGS BREATHE IN AIR. MY BLOOD TAKES OXYGEN FROM THE AIR, AND THEN MY LUNGS BREATHE OUT CARBON DIOXIDE AND WATER VAPOUR.

MUSCLES NEED OXYGEN TO WORK,

4

If I didn't have LUNGS

Some spiders and snails have lungs. But it's difficult to imagine a snail getting out of breath!

The diaphragm, a muscle between the ribs and the stomach, helps the lungs to suck in air. Relaxing, you only breathe in about ten times a minute.

Even plants and trees have to breathe, but they do the opposite to humans. They take in carbon dioxide and water and give out oxygen. We need oxygen to live, so we couldn't do without them.

In an average year, your heart will pump over 36 million times. It beats about 70 times a minute when you are relaxed, and up to 200 times a minute if you are excited.

Y LUNGS AND HEART TAKE CARE OF THIS.

or a

HEART...

MY HEART GETS OXYGEN-RICH BLOOD FROM MY LUNGS AND THEN PUMPS IT TO CELLS IN EVERY PART OF MY BODY.

Earthworms have lots of hearts. It must be quite something when they fall in love.

Hearts don't break, but sometimes it feels like it.

I CAN DO WITHOUT A LOT OF THINGS BUT I CAN'T SURVIVE WITHOUT A HEART OR LUNGS — NOT EVEN FOR FIVE MINUTES.

The great thing about the heart is that you don't have to think about it to make it work — it just gets on with the job.

It would be tricky to have to keep thinking about making your heart beat while trying to do your sums.

The temperature of crocodiles' blood goes up and down as the weather temperature goes up and down. They are called 'cold blooded'. Humans are 'hot blooded' — our blood stays the same whatever the weather.

Normal human body temperature is like a hot summer day — 37°C or 98.6°F.

5

If I didn't have BLOOD.

BLOOD TAKES OXYGEN AND FOOD TO CELLS IN EVERY PART OF MY BODY. IT ALSO GETS RID OF WASTES.

Blood travels around our bodies through a complicated network of blood vessels. Blood gets oxygen in the lungs, goes to the heart, and is then pumped into arteries, then into tiny capillaries.

Ladybirds' blood smells terrible. They squirt it at anything that attacks them.

You have about 100,000 kilometres of blood vessels — put in a line, they would go around the Earth twice!

Blood cells are tiny — but you have about five litres of blood in your body altogether.

O EVERY PART OF MY BODY.

VAMPIRES WOULD GO OUT OF BUSINESS.

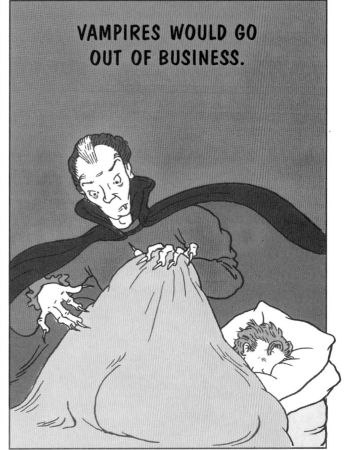

HALF OF MY BLOOD IS MADE UP OF WATERY PLASMA. THIS CARRIES RED AND WHITE CELLS, PLATELETS, FOOD, WASTES AND ANTIBODIES.

Red blood cells carry oxygen around the body.

White blood cells are bigger than red ones and there are fewer of them. They are like soldiers protecting your body — they fight infection, capture and get rid of bacteria, and get worn out in the process.

FOOD GOES FROM MY STOMACH
TO MY SMALL INTESTINE.
HERE, NUTRIENTS ARE TAKEN FROM
THE FOOD AND SENT INTO MY BLOOD.

I COULD ONLY DREAM
ABOUT CHOCOLATE.

Your stomach can hold about one
and a half litres, though some
people seem to manage to put more
in than others.

Pygmy shrews have to eat all the time.
If they don't eat, even for a few
hours, they die...

shrews don't go on long journeys!

If I didn't have a STOMACH

Cows have two stomachs, divided into four
parts. Food goes into the first stomach,
has some juices added, then goes back to
the mouth to be chewed.

Never try kissing a cow!

The starfish is strange — it can turn its
stomach inside out to eat things like
clams. If your stomach did this, you'd
get dinner all over your clothes.

Camels can bring food back up from their stomachs to spit at enemies. Well, you'd certainly back off if someone sprayed chewed stew at you!

An average man eats about 50 tonnes of food during his life. That's about eight and a half elephants — not including pudding.

AS WELL AS OXYGEN.

IN MY STOMACH, FOOD IS CHURNED AND MIXED WITH CHEMICAL JUICES WHICH DIGEST THE FOOD.

Plant-eating dinosaurs like the huge Diplodocus swallowed large stones called 'gizzard stones' which they used to grind up leaves in their stomachs.

After a big meal, food is churned in the stomach for four hours.

All that hard work and then you are hungry again!

SOMETIMES, FOR EXAMPLE IF I HAD AN ACCIDENT, MY BODY MIGHT NOT DIGEST FOOD. NUTRIENTS AND VITAMINS COULD BE TUBE-FED DIRECTLY INTO MY BLOOD.

Saliva, or spit, is a clear fluid which helps us to swallow and digest food. Grown-ups make up to 2 litres of saliva in their mouths every day. Yuck!

An elephant's tusks are actually two huge teeth, and they continue to grow throughout its life.

An elephant probably needs a huge toothbrush.

7

If I didn't have GUMS...

Babies have gums, but no teeth, and have to eat mashed food. However, they don't complain because they can't talk yet.

A jellyfish's mouth is on its underside — must be strange to sit on your mouth!

I'D HAVE TO FIND SOMETHING ELSE TO DO WITH CHEWING GUM.

The tongue of the giant anteater is about 60 cm long and can lick up to 500 ants in one go.

No one has ever measured the size of an ant's tongue as they are usually running away!

THROUGH MY MOUTH.

FOOD BEGINS TO BE BROKEN DOWN IN MY MOUTH. MY TEETH CHOP IT UP AND SALIVA STARTS TO DIGEST IT.

MY TEETH WOULD FALL OUT.

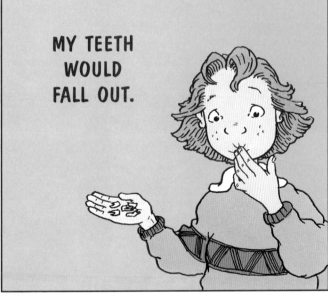

A sea creature called a chiton has its mouth in front of its foot. It doesn't matter where your mouth is as long as you can use it to eat.

Platypus babies have three small teeth which fall out when they grow up. Adult platypus have no teeth at all. They probably have a lousy smile.

Mole rats don't speak — a boy mole rat tells a girl rat he likes her by banging his head against the ceiling of the burrow! Mole rat chemists probably sell lots of pain killers.

When a honey bee finds food, she tells the other bees about it by dancing. She does this without any orchestra to play for her.

Some creatures are all mouth — there's a small sea creature called a lancelet which has no heart, no bones and no eyes.

It does have a mouth, but doesn't have a lot to talk about!

8

If I didn't have a MOUTH...

I COULDN'T GET IN TROUBLE FOR RUNNING UP HUGE PHONE BILLS.

Chimpanzees don't talk, but they do use gestures to communicate. Some chimps have been taught to use human sign language.

I'D BE A LOUSY SINGER.

Dolphins communicate by making high-pitched noises. They can make 200,000 vibrations a second — that's a lot! You wouldn't want to be a baby dolphin having your mother yell at you.

VERY IMPORTANT FUNCTIONS.

I COULDN'T WHISTLE FOR MY DOG.

SOUND STARTS IN THE VOCAL CHORDS IN MY THROAT. IT IS MADE INTO SPEECH BY MY LIPS AND MY TONGUE.

Humpback whales are well known for their singing. Every spring they meet up and sing one song over and over again for hours.

Each spring whales have a new song. Maybe there's a kind of Mozart whale somewhere, writing songs for them.

THE INSIDE OF MY BODY IS MOIST AND SQUISHY. MY SKIN IS A WATERPROOF COVER WHICH PROTECTS MY INSIDES.

Fish and snakes have scales to protect their skin — a bit like your nails, but all over.

I'D HAVE TO WEAR PLASTERS ALL OVER.

If I didn't have SKIN.

Skin cells only live about 24 days, then the dead cells fall off. Most house dust is old flakes of dead skin!

Snakes shed all of their skin in one go. Imagine if you could do that with yours!

Your fingertips have ridges to grip things. Your toes do too but gorillas' toes are better.

Cats don't just feel through their skin, they also use their whiskers. My grandad has whiskers, but he just gets his dinner on them.

MY WHOLE BODY.

I WOULDN'T KNOW IF THE BATH WAS TOO HOT AND I COULD BURN MY BOTTOM!

Some animals can't control their temperature like humans. In the morning, they have to sit in the sun to warm up before they can run about.

I WOULDN'T BE ABLE TO SWEAT SO I MIGHT BOIL OVER.

WHEN I GET HOT, GLANDS IN MY SKIN MAKE SWEAT. THIS HELPS ME TO COOL DOWN.

Instead of sweating, dogs cool down by panting.

Some people are funny about hair — they say hairy legs are OK for men but think women should shave theirs.

Our human ancestors were much hairier than us so the babies could cling to their mothers — like monkeys. Human babies still have this grasping reflex.

The horn of a rhinoceros is not made of bone, it is made of a lot of hairs fused together. You wouldn't want to try combing that!

10

If I didn't have HAIR...

Human body hair doesn't grow all the time otherwise we'd need shearing, like sheep!

Birds have feathers instead of hair, and often use them to attract a mate. Some humans try this with their hair, but it doesn't work as well.

Hair is made of the same stuff as fingernails, except fingernails are much harder — unless you're using the wrong shampoo!

Most people have 100,000 hairs on their head and lose about 60 every day.

Some people lose more than this — and get quite cross about it.

N MY SKIN CALLED FOLLICLES.

Every follicle has a tiny muscle which pulls the hair straight up when you get cold. The hair can then trap a layer of air around the skin to keep it warm.

Humans have most hair on their heads because this is where most heat is lost. Some people wear hats to help stay warm, some wear them just to show off!

The type of hair you have depends on your follicles: oval-shaped ones make wavy hair, flat ones make curly hair and round ones make straight hair. If you don't like your hair, you should blame your follicles.

TINY HAIRS COVER MY WHOLE BODY EXCEPT FOR MY PALMS AND THE SOLES OF MY FEET.

Some starfish make more starfish by detatching one of their arms. This arm grows into a new starfish and the parent then grows a new arm. Sounds painful!

When it is born, a baby kangaroo is tiny and looks a bit like a slug. It crawls up the mother's fur, into a pouch where it grows up.

A baby kangaroo is always called Joey whether it is a boy or a girl.

EVERY HUMAN HAS A TUMMYBUTTON

11

If I didn't have a TUMMY-BUTTON...

Scarab beetles don't have tummy-buttons. The parents roll dung into a ball and push it into a hole with their eggs. When the babies hatch, they feed off the dung.

I'd rather have a tummybutton!

ANIMALS THAT COME FROM EGGS DON'T HAVE TUMMYBUTTONS.

All oysters start life as boys, then slowly they become girls, lay eggs and change back into boys again. It must be tricky for an oyster football team to select an all-boy squad.

The tummybutton is where a tube called the umbilical cord was attached when you were inside your mum. You got your air and food through this tube.

When you were born, you didn't need the umbilical cord so it was cut — leaving only your tummybutton. Since then you've had to eat through your mouth.

I'D HAVE BEEN HATCHED OUT OF AN EGG!

HUMAN BABIES DEVELOP SAFELY BECAUSE THEY ARE PROTECTED INSIDE THEIR MOTHERS.

In humans, one egg cell from the mother fuses with one sperm cell from the father. The fertilised egg then develops into a baby.

The 'midwife toad' father carries the fertilised eggs on his back legs until the baby toads are ready to be born.

WHAT WAS THE QUESTION?

MY BRAINSTEM CONTROLS VITAL FUNCTIONS LIKE HEARTBEAT, DIGESTION AND BREATHING.

Octopuses have big brains. They can be trained to recognize different shapes, but lessons must take place underwater.

Your brain is better than a computer. A computer needs information and programming before it does anything but your brain can deal with things which are completely new.

Some scientists believe that because dinosaurs like Diplodocus had such long necks, they might have had a second brain at the back of their bodies!

THE MOST IMPORTANT PART

If I didn't have a BRAIN...

The cerebrum is the largest part of the brain and is divided into lobes. The lobes at the back control sight, touch and hearing. Those at the front control movement, smell, thought and emotion.

Men usually have bigger brains than women, but that doesn't mean they're smarter.

OF MY BODY IS MY BRAIN.

MY BRAIN IS MADE UP OF THREE MAIN PARTS: BRAINSTEM, CEREBELLUM AND CEREBRUM.

I HAVEN'T GOT A CLUE.

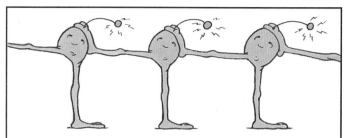

Messages travel through the nervous system by a combination of electrical signals and chemicals which transmit the impulses — just like an electric current moving along a wire.

NO COMMENT.

MY CEREBELLUM COORDINATES MUSCLE MOVEMENT.

The spinal cord carries messages from the nerves to the brain. The brain decides what to do, then sends messages all over your body like your own personal postal system.

Nerves send messages as fast as 100 metres per second — that's quicker than my postman!

Copyright © 1998 Zero to Ten Ltd
Text copyright © 1996 Sandi Toksvig
Illustrations copyright © 1996 David Melling

Edited by Anna McQuinn and Ambreen Husain
Designed by Suzy McGrath and Sarah Godwin

All rights reserved.

First published in Great Britain in 1996
by DeAgostini Editions.
First paperback edition published in 1998
by Zero to Ten Ltd
46 Chalvey Road East
Slough, Berkshire, SL1 2LR

No part of the publication may be reproduced
or utilized in any form or by any means, electronic
or mechanical, including photocopying, recording
or by any information retrieval system, without
the prior written permission of the Publishers.

A CIP catalogue record for this book is available from the British Library

ISBN 1-84089-037-1

Printed and bound in Spain